TOWNSHIP OF
FREE PUBLIC

P9-DLZ-385

BASEBALL LEGENDS

Hank Aaron
Grover Cleveland Alexander
Ernie Banks
Johnny Bench
Yogi Berra
Roy Campanella
Roberto Clemente
Ty Cobb
Dizzy Dean
Joe DiMaggio
Bob Feller
Jimmie Foxx
Lou Gehrig
Bob Gibson
Rogers Hornsby
Walter Johnson
Sandy Koufax
Mickey Mantle
Christy Mathewson
Willie Mays
Stan Musial
Satchel Paige
Brooks Robinson
Frank Robinson
Jackie Robinson
Babe Ruth
Duke Snider
Warren Spahn
Willie Stargell
Honus Wagner
Ted Williams
Carl Yastrzemski
Cy Young

CHELSEA HOUSE PUBLISHERS

BASEBALL LEGENDS

ROY CAMPANELLA

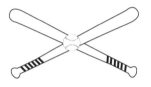

James Tackach

Introduction by
Jim Murray

Senior Consultant
Earl Weaver

CHELSEA HOUSE PUBLISHERS
New York • Philadelphia

TOWNSHIP OF UNION
FREE PUBLIC LIBRARY

Published by arrangement with
Chelsea House Publishers.
Newfield Publications is a federally
registered trademark of Newfield
Publications, Inc.

Produced by James Charlton Associates
New York, New York.

Designed by Hudson Studio
Ossining, New York.

Typesetting by LinoGraphics
New York, New York.

Picture research by Carolann Hawkins
Cover illustration by Dan O'Leary

Copyright © 1991 by Chelsea House Publishers, a division of Main
Line Book Co. All rights reserved. Printed and bound in the United
States of America.

Library of Congress Cataloging-in-Publication Data

Tackach, James.
  Roy Campanella / James Tackach ; introduction by Jim Murray.
    p. cm.—(Baseball legends)
  Includes bibliographical references.
  Summary: Examines the life of the baseball player whose successful
career with the Brooklyn Dodgers was ended by a serious automobile
accident.
  ISBN 0-7910-1170-4.—ISBN 0-7910-1204-2 (pbk.)
  1. Campanella, Roy, 1921- —Juvenile literature. 2. Baseball
players—United States—Biography—Juvenile literature.
[1. Capanella, Roy, 1921- . 2. Baseball players.] I. Title.
II. Series.
GV865.C3T33 1990
796.357'092—dc20
[B]
                              90-33856
                                    CIP

$ 14.95

JB
CAMPANELLA, R
c. 1

CONTENTS

WHAT MAKES A STAR

Jim Murray

No one has ever been able to explain to me the mysterious alchemy that makes one man a .350 hitter and another player, more or less identical in physical makeup, hard put to hit .200. You look at an Al Kaline, who played with the Detroit Tigers from 1953 to 1974. He was pale, stringy, almost poetic-looking. He always seemed to be struggling against a bad case of mononucleosis. But with a bat in his hands, he was King Kong. During his career, he hit 399 home runs, rapped out 3,007 hits, and compiled a .297 batting average.

Form isn't the reason. The first time anybody saw Roberto Clemente step into the batter's box for the Pittsburgh Pirates, the best guess was that Clemente would be back in Double A ball in a week. He had one foot in the bucket and held his bat at an awkward angle—he looked as though he couldn't hit an outside pitch. A lot of other ballplayers may have had a better-looking stance. Yet they never led the National League in hitting in four different years, the way Clemente did.

Not every ballplayer is born with the ability to hit a curveball. Nor is exceptional hand-eye coordination the key to heavy hitting. Big-league locker rooms are filled with players who have all the attributes, save one: discipline. Every baseball man can tell you a story about a pitcher who throws a ball faster than anyone has ever seen but who has no control on or *off* the field.

The Hall of Fame is full of people who transformed themselves into great ballplayers by working at the sport, by studying the game, and making sacrifices. They're overachievers—and winners. If you want to find them, just watch the World Series. Or simply read about New York Yankee great Lou Gehrig; Ted Williams, "the Splendid Splinter" of the Boston Red Sox; or the Dodgers' strikeout king Sandy Koufax.

A pitcher *should* be able to win a lot of ballgames with a 98-miles-per-hour fastball. But what about the pitcher who wins 20 games a year with a fastball so slow that you can catch it with your teeth? Bob Feller of the Cleveland Indians got into the Hall of Fame with a blazing fastball that glowed in the dark. National League star Grover Cleveland Alexander got there with a pitch that took considerably longer to reach the plate; but when it did arrive, the pitch was exactly where Alexander wanted it to be— and the last place the batter expected it to be.

There are probably more players with exceptional ability who didn't make it to the major leagues than there are who did. A number of great hitters, bored with fielding practice, had to be dropped from their team because their home-run production didn't make up for their lapses in the field. And then there are players like Brooks Robinson of the Baltimore Orioles, who made himself into a human vacuum cleaner at third base because he knew that working hard to become an expert fielder would win him a job in the big leagues.

A star is not something that flashes through the sky. That's a comet. Or a meteor. A star is something you can steer ships by. It stays in place and gives off a steady glow; it is fixed, permanent. A star works at being a star.

And that's how you tell a star in baseball. He shows up night after night and takes pride in how brightly he shines. He's Willie Mays running so hard his hat keeps falling off; Ty Cobb sliding to stretch a single into a double; Lou Gehrig, after being fooled in his first two at-bats, belting the next pitch off the light tower because he's taken the time to study the pitcher. Stars never take themselves for granted. That's why they're stars.

1

A CALL FROM THE DODGERS

Through the end of World War II, Roy Campanella followed the same pattern as most black American baseball players. Denied the opportunity to play in the major leagues, they suited up for teams in the all-black Negro Leagues from spring through autumn, then headed down to Cuba for winter ball. Campanella enjoyed living on the road and playing ball year-round. He expected to maintain that schedule for many years to come.

But in 1942, Campanella heard a rumor that, if true, would greatly affect his career. With so many major-league players serving in the armed forces, some people began to suggest that blacks might finally be invited to play on major-league teams. Campanella dismissed the rumors as gossip. "Never once did it occur to me that I would someday be playing in the majors," he wrote in his autobiography years later. "As far as I was concerned, the big leagues were as far away as Siberia."

One spring day in 1945, however, with the war

Even as a young player with the Baltimore Elite Giants in the Negro Leagues, Campanella displayed a home-run swing.

still going on, all that changed. The 23-year-old Campanella was watching batting practice before a Philadelphia Phillies game at Shibe Park when he spotted Phils manager Hans Lobert in the grandstand. He decided to approach Lobert, whom he knew fairly well.

"You can use a catcher," Campanella said. "And I'm a good catcher. I can help this club!"

"Campy," replied Lobert, "when I tell you there's nothing I could use more and better than *you* right now, I'm not kidding you. But I haven't heard any talk about any bars being lowered," he added, referring to the unwritten rule keeping blacks out of the majors. Even so, Lobert gave Campanella the phone number of the club president, Gerry Nugent.

Campanella called Nugent and made the same offer he had made to Lobert. "After nine years with the Baltimore Elite Giants, I'm ready," he said. But Nugent gave Campanella no encouragement. Yes, he knew of Campanella's skills, but he also knew he could not change long-standing baseball policy overnight.

Campanella put the idea out of his mind and continued playing with the Elites. But after the 1945 season ended, he got another chance to offer his services to the major leagues. Just before heading to Venezuela for winter ball, he was invited by the owner of the Newark Eagles to play on an all-star team with other Negro League stars against a group of major-leaguers. A five-game series would be played in Brooklyn and Newark. Campanella agreed to take part and looked forward to competing against some of baseball's biggest stars

After one of the games, Chuck Dressen, manager of the major-league team, took the catcher aside. Dressen, a coach with the Brooklyn Dodgers, explained that Dodger president

Branch Rickey wanted to meet Campanella the next day at the Dodgers' office in Brooklyn.

When Campanella arrived at Rickey's office, he was surprised to find the Dodgers' executive studying a loose-leaf binder filled with information about Campanella's career. It included reports from teachers who had had Campanella in class as well as rating sheets from scouts who had seen him play.

"I've investigated dozens of players in the Negro Leagues," Rickey said. "I've tried to learn as much as I could about their personal habits, their family life, their early childhood, their education, their social activities, practically everything there is to know about them." He went on to praise Campanella as a hard worker who

Branch Rickey, the Brooklyn Dodgers' president, who first signed Jackie Robinson to a major-league contract, soon had Campanella in Dodger blue as well.

got along well with teammates and coaches. Finally, Rickey asked, "You like to play with me?"

Campanella, who had heard that Rickey was about to establish a Negro team called the Brown Dodgers, assumed the offer applied to that club.

"Mr. Rickey," he said, "I'm one of the highest-paid players in the colored league. I earn around three thousand a year, and I make around two thousand playing winter ball in Puerto Rico, Venezuela, and Cuba. I've worked for the same man for nine years. I like the man. I'm doing all right." Campanella had no intention of giving all that up to play in another Negro League that might not be successful. Still, he promised to stay in touch with Rickey in the future.

A week later, on a road trip, Campanella crossed paths at his hotel with a young player from the Kansas City Monarchs who had built himself quite a reputation as a rookie in the Negro American League. His name was Jackie Robinson. Campanella had played in an all-star game against Robinson, and he remembered that the youngster had gotten four hits and had run the bases smartly. Negro Leaguers were comparing Robinson to the legendary Ty Cobb.

Robinson asked Campanella to come with him to his room for a card game. Campanella agreed, but Robinson did not really want to play cards. In the privacy of his hotel room, he revealed that two months earlier he had signed a contract with Branch Rickey.

Campanella shook his head. "You can take a chance with a new league," he said. "But it's like I told Mr. Rickey, I can't afford to."

"I didn't sign with the Brown Dodgers," Robinson said, much to Campanella's surprise. "I'm going to play for Montreal." Montreal was the top-level

Dodger farm team. "I'm going to be the first Negro in organized baseball," Robinson flatly announced.

Campanella promised to keep the news secret, but the next day, October 23, 1945, Robinson traveled to Montreal for a press conference with Rickey. The story made headlines all over the country. Baseball's color line would soon be broken.

Now Campanella worried that his lack of enthusiasm during his talk with Branch Rickey might have cost him a shot with the Dodgers. But that winter Rickey sent a telegram to Campanella in Venezuela. It read: PLEASE REPORT BROOKLYN OFFICE BY MARCH 10 VERY IMPORTANT. BRANCH RICKEY.

2

THE KID FROM NICETOWN

The Roy Campanella story began in Homestead, Pennsylvania, where Roy, the youngest of John and Ida Campanella's four children, was born on November 19, 1921. When Roy was 7 years old, the family moved to a section of North Philadelphia called Nicetown. It was a pleasant working-class neighborhood inhabited by Polish, Italian, and black families. Roy's father was Italian, and his mother was black.

John Campanella made his living peddling vegetables and fish. Each morning, with Roy's help, he loaded his truck and traveled from neighborhood to neighborhood selling his produce. Every Friday, he purchased several cases of fresh fish and sold them to the Catholic families who did not eat meat on Fridays.

By the time Roy was 12 years old, he, too, was working. He awoke at 2 o'clock each morning to

Campanella and Sammy Hughes (left), teammates on the Baltimore Elite Giants. Hughes was considered the premier second baseman in the Negro Leagues, but by the time organized baseball opened up for blacks, he was well past his prime. In 10 exhibition games against major leaguers, Hughes hit .390.

complete a milk route for the Supplee Dairy. He drove a horse-drawn wagon and delivered milk and other dairy products to all his customers. Then he came home to help his father load the vegetable truck before hurrying to school. Roy received 25 cents per day for delivering milk, but he did not keep it. All his money went to his mother, who used it to buy school clothes for Roy. These were the 1930s, the years of the Great Depression, when money was hard to come by. Mrs. Campanella needed every dollar to keep her family clothed and fed.

When Roy was 13, his older brother, Lawrence, hired him to help on his own milk route. Lawrence used a truck for deliveries, and Roy was driving it before his 14th birthday. When he was not delivering milk or attending school, Roy hustled nickels and dimes by shining shoes and selling newspapers on the street.

On Sundays, however, no one in the Campanella family worked. Every Sunday morning, Mrs. Campanella took her children to the local Baptist church for services. Sometimes, John Campanella, who was a Catholic, accompanied the family. Whenever he entered the church, the whole congregation would turn and stare at him. Roy had no idea why they did that. Only later did he realize that his father was the only white man in the building.

As a young child, Roy had no idea that his parents were of different races—they were simply his parents. But eventually Roy's classmates began to tease him about his heritage. They called him and his sister Doris "halfbreeds." When Doris told Roy what the word meant, he decided to discuss the matter with his mother. Mrs. Campanella was in the kitchen ironing one

Campanella stayed close to his parents even after he was an all-star with the Brooklyn Dodgers. In 1954, Roy and his parents read from the family bible, the same bible Mrs. Campanella had been reading to her son since he was a baby.

of her husband's shirts when Roy came home from school that day.

"Mom, is it true that Daddy is a white man?" he asked.

Mrs. Campanella stiffened a bit, then addressed her son softly but firmly. "Yes, Roy, your father is white," she said. "It makes no difference. There's nothing wrong with that. He's a good man. And above all, he gives us what many folks, white or colored, can't buy with all the money in the world. He gives us love, Roy. What more can anyone want?"

Roy never brought up the subject again. And he soon learned to ignore the insults from others. Furthermore, by the time he was in junior high school, Roy had developed into a strong, sturdily built youngster. He was a member of the Wissahickon Boys Club boxing team and a Golden Gloves competitor, so the word quickly spread that good-natured Roy Campanella from Nicetown was not someone to rile.

Future Hall of Famer Josh Gibson scores in the 1944 Negro League All-Star game in Chicago's Comiskey Park. In 13 complete seasons in the Negro Leagues, Gibson won 9 home run titles and 4 batting crowns.

Despite his success in boxing, Roy's favorite sport was baseball. On the wall in his room hung pictures of Mickey Cochrane of the hometown Philadelphia Athletics, Bill Dickey, Babe Ruth, and Lou Gehrig of the New York Yankees. He also had photos of the great Negro League stars: Satchel Paige and Josh Gibson of the Pittsburgh Crawfords and Biz Mackey of the Baltimore Elite Giants.

Roy was an avid fan. At World Series time, he would rush home from school and position himself in front of the family radio to hear the broadcasts of the games. In 1933 he listened intently as Carl Hubbell, the New York Giants' great screwballer,

tamed Joe Cronin's Washington Senators. As batter after batter went down swinging, he imagined himself catching Hubbell's tricky pitches.

Roy saw his first games at Philadelphia's Shibe Park, where Connie Mack's Athletics played. Although Roy could not afford to pay 50 cents for a bleacher seat, for a quarter the superintendent of an apartment building near the park allowed him to sit on the roof and watch the game.

Roy played stickball before he ever played baseball. He and his friends sawed off the bristles of an old broom and used the handle as a bat. Their ball was made of red rubber with dimples on the whole surface—a "pimple ball" they called it—and gloves were unnecessary.

When Roy finally began playing hardball, he desperately wanted a glove. One day while walking through a neighborhood park, he saw one lying a short distance from the baseball diamond. Some boys were playing a game, but no one seemed to be using the mitt. Roy swiped it, brought it home, and hid it in the china closet. His mother found it two days later. When she demanded to know where the glove came from, Roy claimed he had found it in the park. Sensing that she was not getting the full story, Mrs. Campanella insisted Roy return the glove to the exact spot where he found it.

In sandlot games, Roy often ended up behind the plate—with a friend's borrowed mitt. He was a stocky youngster, and it was just assumed that the biggest kid on the field was supposed to catch. Roy's only problem as a catcher was that the mask distracted him; when he wore one he could not seem to follow the pitch into his glove, so he began to play without one.

One day, a batter foul-tipped a ball right into Roy's face, and a stream of blood began flowing from his nose. By the time he got home, the nose was swollen to twice its normal size.

John Campanella had not wanted Roy to play hardball because he thought the game was too dangerous, so when he saw Roy's nose at suppertime, he was not pleased. When he questioned Roy about the injury, Roy's sister Gladys supplied the answer. "He was catching again, Dad," she said. Then she added, "And without a mask. Can you imagine anyone so stupid?" From then on, Roy caught with a mask.

Roy played on his first organized team when he was 12 years old. The Philadelphia *Independent*, the newspaper Roy sold on street corners, sponsored a team for the Nicetown Colored Athletic Club. The NCAC was organized because in those days black youngsters were prohibited from joining the local Boys Club. Most of the boys on the team were older than Roy, so he did not play very often. But he loved wearing the clean white uniform and watching the games from the bench.

At Gillespie Junior High, Roy got the chance to play organized ball more regularly. On tryout day, a chilly afternoon in early March, the baseball coach assembled the would-be players in the gymnasium and told them to divide themselves according to the positions they played. He told the pitchers to congregate in one area, infielders in another, and outfielders in another. As the groups started forming, Roy noticed that no one headed for the spot designated for catchers. Although he had caught on the sandlots, he had no great love for catching; squatting in the dirt with all that equipment was tiring. Still, he headed straight for the spot marked for catchers. With no competition, he felt sure he would make the team.

Actually, Roy would have made the team at any

Biz Mackey, Negro League great, taught Campanella much of what he knew about catching. Monte Irvin, who played with Mackey, said of him: "He was the dean of teachers. He taught Campanella how to think like a catcher, how to set a hitter up—throw a hitter his favorite pitch at a time when he's not expecting it."

position. His years of stickball and sandlot hardball had made him a smart and solid hitter. He had developed a powerful swing that propelled the ball to the far reaches of the outfield when he made good contact. And in spite of his size, he ran well— fast enough to make the track team at Simon Gratz High School two years later.

By the time Roy reached high school, he had earned a reputation as one of the best young athletes in the Philadelphia area. At the age of 15, he was playing sandlot ball against men in their early 20s and holding his own. That summer, he was invited to play for Loudensluger Post 366 in the American Legion League. No black youngster had ever before been asked to join the squad.

It was after an American Legion contest that Roy met Tom Dixon, a catcher on the Bacharach Giants, a Philadelphia-based black semi-pro team that also played in New York and New Jersey.

"Would you like to play for the Bacharach Giants?" Dixon asked. Roy could hardly believe his ears.

"Well, I'd sure like to," Roy answered, "but I've never traveled anyplace. My folks would never leave me travel out of the city—sleep away from home and all that. I'd sure like to play on your team, but I'm afraid my mother wouldn't let me."

The next day, Dixon paid Mrs. Campanella a visit. After explaining that Roy would play for the Giants only on weekends and therefore would not miss any school, he assured her that Roy would eat well and lodge in decent hotels any time the team stayed overnight. He also promised to take her son to church with him on Sundays. "We have an honest, God-fearing bunch of boys and we play an honest game of ball," he said. "No cussing, no swearing, no gambling." Finally, he explained that Roy would receive $35 for two weekend games—to be paid directly to Mrs. Campanella.

Now it was Mrs. Campanella who could not believe her ears. This was the spring of 1937, and that $35 was more than her husband made for a whole week's work. The deal was made, and Roy Campanella became a professional ballplayer.

But Roy's career with the Bacharach Giants ended after only three games. He played in Beach Haven, New Jersey, on Friday night and stayed with the club at the Woodside Hotel in Harlem until Sunday, when the Giants were scheduled to travel to Hartford, Connecticut. Also at the Woodside were the Baltimore Elite Giants of the Negro National League. On Sunday morning after breakfast, Biz Mackey, Baltimore's catcher-manager, approached Tom Dixon and Roy. Mackey was a veteran of almost two decades of Negro League baseball.

"Tom," he said. "I need a catcher—a good young kid I can break in to give me a rest. I'm beginnin' to get beat. You know anyone?"

Dixon introduced Roy, and Mackey immediately offered him a job. He had heard about the big catcher from Nicetown. Roy honored his commitment to play with the Giants in Hartford, but he promised to call Mackey during the week.

On Tuesday, Mackey made Roy an offer: $60 per month plus expenses. After promising to discuss the deal with his mother, Roy played again that night for the Bacharach Giants.

The next day, Mackey and Tom Wilson, the owner of the Elites, visited Mrs. Campanella and worked out a deal. Roy would play locally with the team on weekends until June, when school was out, and then play full-time and travel with the team. Mrs. Campanella would receive the $60 per month salary, and Roy would keep the expense money.

Top Row

...co Chataing Roy Campanella Marvin Barker Bill Anderson

...ge Jefferson Parnell Woods Roy Welmaker Buck Leonard,

...e Robinson Eugene Benson Felton Snow Verdel Mathis Sam
Mgr. Camp
...rican All Stars

3

LIFE IN THE NEGRO LEAGUES

In the summer of 1937, when Roy Campanella joined the Baltimore Elite Giants, many schools and businesses were racially segregated, and so were the United States armed forces, with separate battalions for white and black servicemen. In the South, hotels, restaurants, and stores were segregated. Baseball teams followed this practice as well.

The Baltimore Elite Giants were part of the Negro National League, which included teams in the East. The Negro American League operated in the South and Midwest. These two leagues offered the highest level of competition for black ballplayers. In 1937, the top players were future Hall of Famers Josh Gibson, Satchel Paige, Judy Johnson, and Buck Leonard.

The black teams generally played between 150 and 200 games in the United States during the spring, summer, and autumn, then headed to

Campanella (top, 2nd from left) and other Negro League stars travelled widely to play baseball. This Caracas, Venezuela, team in 1945 included Buck Leonard, a future Hall of Famer, and two future National League Rookies of the year, Jackie Robinson and Sam Jethroe.

Puerto Rico, Mexico, or South America to play another 50 or 100 games during the winter.

Like most other Negro League teams, the Elite Giants owned a team bus—a blue and white one, with the team name stenciled along its sides—that transported the players from town to town. If the team was traveling in the South and the driver could not find a hotel that was willing to lodge black travelers, he would pull over to the side of the road and the bus would function as a hotel. Sometimes the bus served as a restaurant and locker room as well. On long trips, the players passed the time playing cards, telling stories, and talking baseball.

Having spent his whole life in and around Philadelphia, Campanella was thrilled with this opportunity to travel and see the country. The schedule was grueling—he caught two double-headers almost every Sunday and once caught three doubleheaders in one day—but he loved the entire experience. At first, Campanella played second-string to Biz Mackey, but the young catcher's playing time increased quickly as he proved himself a capable receiver. Mackey taught him how to catch the quick-dropping spitballs that the Negro League pitchers loved to throw and how to pick out the weak spot in a batter's stroke in order to call for the appropriate pitch.

As he got more and more at-bats, Campanella's hitting also improved. He now weighed almost 190 pounds, and he was still growing and filling out. When he connected solidly with a pitch, the ball traveled a long way.

Campanella returned home in September, determined to make his living playing baseball. He was not a bad student, but after traveling with the Elites, his schoolwork did not seem very interesting. He asked his parents if he could quit

In 1942 and 1943, Campanella played for the Monterrey team in Mexico.

school and play full-time with the Elites.

John Campanella did not want his son to quit school; he believed that an education could open doors for Roy that had been closed to himself. But this was 1937, the middle of the Great Depression, and almost one-third of the American work force was unemployed. Even if he graduated from high school, Roy reasoned, he might not be able to find a suitable job.

Mrs. Campanella pleaded her son's case. "Roy is a smart boy," she told her husband. "Maybe that Negro League isn't the best there is. But it sure isn't the worst there is, either. They pay our boy good, real good. And in time he can earn more money than he could in any other line. And to love what you're doing...that's important, too."

Roy Campanella left school in November 1937, immediately after his 16th birthday, and told Tom Wilson that he would be ready to join the Elite

Giants on March 20th in Nashville, Tennessee, for spring training. On St. Patrick's Day, Campanella boarded a Nashville-bound train in Philadelphia. He was eager to begin his first full professional season. He would receive a salary of $90 per month.

That spring and summer, Campanella played all over the country. As a full-time Elite, Roy was no longer playing second-string to Biz Mackey. He shared catching duties with the veteran backstop and patiently listened as Mackey passed along advice. One of the first things Mackey taught his young student was to cut down on his swing in order to make contact more frequently. "Don't kill the ball," he told Roy. "Just meet it. It'll go plenty far!"

At the end of the 1938 season, Tom Wilson traded Mackey to Newark and made Roy the team's first-string catcher. The move paid off. Campanella had a fine season, and so did the Elites. At the season's end, the league's top four teams met in a championship playoff. The Elites beat Newark in the first round, and Homestead eliminated Philadelphia. In the playoff finals, Campanella had the privilege of playing against one of his boyhood idols: Josh Gibson.

Gibson, too, was a catcher—and the greatest power hitter (in 1931, he had smashed 75 home runs) who ever played Negro League baseball. Many called him "the black Babe Ruth." He was 6'2" and weighed 230 pounds, with huge arms and barrel-chested. In Gibson's time, home runs were rarely paced off for distance, but one of his blasts in Monessen, Pennsylvania, was so impressive that the mayor ordered it measured. It had traveled 512 feet.

But the 1939 Negro National League championship playoffs belonged to Campanella. In one game, he got 5 hits, and he finished the four-game series with 7 runs batted in as the Elite Giants triumphed, 3 games to 1.

That season, Campanella's salary was raised to $120 per month, and he was promised another raise effective the following season. Feeling financially secure, Campanella married his Philadelphia girlfriend, Bernice Ray. A year later, the young couple had their first child, Joyce. Another daughter, Beverly, was born the next year.

With a family to support, Roy worked all year round. He played with the Elites from March to October and when the Negro League season ended, he traveled to Puerto Rico or Cuba for winter ball. In 1941 he was named the all-star catcher for the Negro Nationals. In the game, played in Chicago's Comiskey Park, Campanella managed only one hit, but he excelled in the field. He nailed a hopeful base-stealer in the 2nd inning and picked a runner off second base in the 5th. Twice he threw out baserunners on sacrifice bunt attempts. For his splendid defensive work, he was voted its Most Valuable Player.

Before the 1942 season, the 19-year-old Campanella left the Elite Giants to play for more money in Mexico. He did the same the following spring, but returned to the Elites for 1944 with a hefty raise.

As the 1944 season approached, Campanella was a very satisfied baseball player. He was the best catcher in the Negro Leagues, and including his winter-ball salary, his yearly earnings were more than $5,000. Although many men his age were fighting in World War II, Campanella had received a draft deferment because he was a father.

4

"I'M A BALLPLAYER"

Roy Campanella spent the next two and a half years playing semi-pro ball in the United States and abroad. Although he loved to play ball, the constant travel soon caused him and Bernice to grow apart. Eventually, they divorced. In the winter of 1945, Campanella married for the second time, wedding Ruthe Willis.

That same winter, Campanella received the telegram from Branch Rickey telling him to report to the Brooklyn Dodgers' office by March 10. When the date drew near, Campanella packed his gear and took off for Brooklyn. Rickey was not at the Dodgers' office when Campanella arrived, but an assistant, Bob Finch, informed him that he was trying to find a spot for the young catcher on one of the Dodgers' farm teams. In front of Campanella, Finch called the president of the Danville, Illinois, club. After a brief conversation, Finch hung up.

"They don't want me?" Campanella asked.

"Nope," said Finch. "They don't want you."

Finch then called the Nashua, New Hampshire, team, where Buzzie Bavasi was the man in charge. "Buzzie is one of the finest young fellows in the

Campanella shows his injured hand to Dodgers' manager Walter Alston. When Roy played his first minor league season with the Nashua Dodgers, Alston was Nashua's player-manager.

organization," Finch told Campanella. "He's smart and progressive. You'll like him." Rickey had intended to pair Campanella with a big, hard-throwing Negro League pitcher named Don Newcombe, and Finch asked Bavasi if he was interested in having the two players on the Nashua squad. Bavasi answered straightforwardly: "If they can play ball better than what we have, then we don't care what color they are."

Two days later, Campanella and Newcombe were on a train to New Hampshire.

Nashua, New Hampshire, was a pleasant New England town, and Campanella and Newcombe were easily accepted there, even though they were the town's only black residents. They had no trouble finding housing and did not encounter any prejudice in stores or restaurants. Their biggest complaint was that the local barber had never cut black people's hair. He almost scalped the two players on several occasions.

If any of Nashua's residents harbored any hidden prejudice, they soon changed their mind when they saw Campanella and Newcombe on the diamond. In his first Nashua game, Campanella unloaded a 440-foot homer. And Newcombe soon impressed the hometown fans with his unhittable fastball.

But no one was more impressed than Nashua's manager, Walter Alston. One day, he asked Campanella whether he would be willing to take charge of the team if Alston were tossed out of a game. "Roy," he said, "you're a little bit older than the other fellows on the club, and a great deal more experienced. They respect you."

Those were flattering words, and Campanella only hoped they were true. He got his chance to find out how true they were in mid-June, when Alston was thrown out of the game for arguing a call in the 6th inning, with his team trailing by two runs. The next inning, Campanella sent Newcombe up to pinch-hit with a runner on base. A great-hitting pitcher, Newcombe whacked a long home run into the river beyond the right-field fence to tie the score. Nashua then put together two more runs to win the game.

But Nashua's new black players did encounter some problems around the league. In one game against the Manchester Giants, an opposing batsman picked up a handful of dirt and threw it

Don Newcombe (left) played in the Negro Leagues and was Campanella's team-mate in Nashua and Brooklyn. "Big Newk" is the only player to win Rookie of the Year, MVP and Cy Young awards.

Campanella Best Receiver In NE League Claim Scouts

Roy Campanella, 24 years old, married, father of two daughters, 5 and 6 years old, and a son 2 years old, is a cinch to be the Nashua Dodger first string receiver. There's nothing in the league that can touch him, is the unanimous opinion of Dodger scouts.

Born and raised in Philadelphia, Roy first began to play ball when 14 years old. His first year

out, he caught regularly with a Philly American Legion Junior nine. He played American Legion ball for two seasons, then decided to move up a notch.

That step upward was to move into the Negro National league, with the Baltimore club. There, since 1938, he has played every year with the exception of 1942 and 1943, when he played with Monterey in the Mexican league. Incidentally, Roy was runner-up in home runs in the Mexican loop, with a total of 13.

With a family of four to support, however, the lure of more money brought Campanella back to the Negro National league, and back to Baltimore. He's played there summers ever since. Unfortunately, the league kept no records until 1944. In '44, however, Roy hit a lusty .350. In '45, he improved some. Quite a sum in fact. He hit .365, led the league in runs batted in with 132, finished the season second to Leonard of the Grays in home runs hit with 32. Leonard belted 34.

Roy's baseball seasons have been longer than those played by most ball players. In fact, during the past five years he has played the year round. In the summer it was with the Negro loop, in the winter with either the South American league, the Cuban league or in Puerto Rico. This past winter he played with Vargas in Lefty Gomez' South American league. However the South American loop, like the Negro National and the Mexican, lacks capable instructors, bemoans Campanella.

As a baseball playing "tourist," Campanella is firm in his belief that the only ball that can come close to touching American baseball is that played in Cuba. "It's very fast there," he said.

According to Roy, Nashua is one of the finest towns he's ever had the pleasure of seeing. However, he adds, "the ball park is v-e-r-y large. I'm not going to try for home runs here. The park's much too big."

A clipping from the Nashua, New Hampshire newspaper in 1946 talks about the hot young catching prospect.

in Campanella's face. The generally mild-mannered catcher tossed his mask aside and drew himself up to his full height. "Try that again," he said, "and I'll beat you to a pulp." Needless to say, the Manchester player decided *not* to try it.

Later in the season, after Campanella and Newcombe had helped Nashua beat the Lynn Red Sox, Buzzie Bavasi was collecting Nashua's share of the gate receipts when Lynn's general manager remarked, "If it wasn't for them niggers, you wouldn't have beat us." Unlike Campanella, Bavasi gave no warning—he simply charged the man, and players from both teams had to come in to break up the ensuing battle.

Campanella finished the season with 14 homers, 96 RBIs, and a .290 batting average. In addition, he led the league's catchers in putouts and assists and stole 10 bases. For his efforts, Campanella was named the league's MVP.

The next year, 1947, Jackie Robinson made history as the first black major leaguer. Meanwhile,

Campanella played with Montreal, Robinson's former team. Although his hitting tailed off late in the summer, Campanella still batted .273 and won another league MVP award. And by 1948 he felt ready to play in Brooklyn.

But Branch Rickey had other plans for his talented young catcher. He wanted to integrate the American Association, the AAA league in which the Dodgers had a farm club. Campanella played only three games in Brooklyn before reluctantly departing to the Dodgers' St. Paul franchise. He did not like being sent to the minors merely to integrate a league. "I'm a ballplayer, not a pioneer," he told Branch Rickey.

Campanella quickly proved how overqualified he was for AAA baseball. In 35 games with St. Paul, he batted .325 and drove in 39 runs. Half his hits were for extra bases. Meanwhile, the Dodgers were floundering in seventh place. In late June, they summoned Campanella back to Brooklyn.

In his first game, on July 2nd, Campanella hit a double and 2 singles. The next day, he tripled and banged 2 more singles. In his third game, he homered twice. Sparked by their rookie catcher, the Dodgers won 16 of 19 games.

Brooklyn finished the 1948 season in third place, $7^1/_2$ games behind the front-running Boston Braves. In his half season, Roy Campanella had hit 9 homers and driven home 45 runs. He was in the major leagues to stay.

"The Boys of Summer," the fabled infield of the Brooklyn Dodgers in the early 1950s; (clockwise from left) Robinson, Hodges, Campanella, Cox, and Reese.

The Brooklyn Dodgers squad that Roy Campanella joined for spring training in 1949 developed into a great team. Campanella became the starting catcher. The infield consisted of Gil Hodges at first base, Jackie Robinson at second, Pee Wee Reese at shortstop, and Billy Cox at third. Duke Snider played center field, and Carl Furillo played right. The pitching staff included Preacher Roe, Carl Erskine, and Don Newcombe. After their careers ended, Robinson, Reese, Snider, and Campanella would all be elected to baseball's Hall of Fame.

The team played at Ebbets Field, a cozy old ballpark in the Flatbush section of Brooklyn, New York. Its outfield dimensions were not uniform, often causing long fly balls to take weird bounces off the irregularly shaped walls. The Dodgers' fans, like the team itself, were a diverse group. Jews, blacks, Italians, and Poles were just some of the people who found their way to Ebbets Field.

Because the Dodgers were the first major-league team to integrate, both their black and white players were subjected to racist slurs by

Ebbets Field, home of the Brooklyn Dodgers from 1913 until 1958, when the team moved to Los Angeles. The cozy ball park, beloved in Brooklyn, had a right-field fence just 297 feet from home plate.

opposing dugouts. They suffered intentional spike wounds and withstood brushback pitches. But these attempts to injure the players served only to strengthen team unity. Whenever Robinson, Newcombe, and Campanella were barred from joining the rest of the team in a restaurant or hotel, their white teammates became outraged. This anger fueled a fierce desire to win.

And win they did. The Brooklyn Dodgers captured the 1949 National League pennant, beating out the St. Louis Cardinals by a single game. Robinson batted .342 and won the MVP award. Hodges and Furillo each drove in more than 100 runs, Newcombe won 17 times and received the Rookie of the Year Award, and Campanella batted a solid .287 with 22 homers. In the World Series, however, manager Casey Stengel's strong New York Yankee team outplayed the Dodgers, 4 games to 1.

The 1949 season set a pattern that would be repeated again and again over the next several years: a splendid Brooklyn team would fall just short of a world championship. In 1950, the Dodgers and the Philadelphia Phillies dueled through the September pennant run. The two teams met for the last few games of the season. Going into the final game at Ebbets Field, Philadelphia was one game ahead in the standings. A Dodger win would tie things, with a post-season playoff needed to decide the pennant. The Dodgers made a valiant effort through nine well-played innings, then finally lost the game—and another shot at the Series—when the Phils pulled ahead in the 10th.

The 1951 season brought even more bitter disappointment. The Dodgers got off to a great start and were $13\frac{1}{2}$ games ahead by mid-August. Surely, it seemed, no one would catch them. But slumps and injuries made the team stumble just as the rival New York Giants began a super winning streak. The Giants actually took the lead in the season's final days, but this time a dramatic 9-8 extra-inning Dodger victory on the last day of the season left the teams tied for first place. A three-game playoff was held to decide the pennant.

The teams split the first two playoff games. In the third game, the Dodgers were ahead 4–2 in the bottom of the 9th. Then, with one out and two Giant runners on base, Brooklyn manager Chuck Dressen removed Newcombe from the game and brought Ralph Branca in to pitch. Campanella, sidelined by an injury, could only watch helplessly from the bench as Bobby Thomson lined Branca's second pitch into the left-field seats to give the Giants the National League pennant.

Though the 1950 and 1951 seasons were bitter ones for the Dodgers and their fans, no one could complain about Campanella's contributions to the team. In 1950, he batted .281 and smacked 31 home runs. And in 1951 he performed even better: a .325 average, 33 homers, and 108 RBIs. These

1952 Wheaties Card.

statistics made him the sportswriters' choice as the league's Most Valuable Player.

In addition to his fine work at the plate and behind it, the hard-hitting catcher was developing into a true team leader. Campanella's teammates began calling him the "Good Humor Man" because of his good-natured personality. In the locker room and on train rides, they egged him on to recount some of his experiences in the Negro Leagues, and he soon became the team's best storyteller. On the field, he chattered cheerfully with teammates, umpires, and opposing hitters, keeping everybody loose and tuned in to the game.

Campanella sometimes roomed with Jackie Robinson, but the two black men dealt with their situations very differently. When someone insulted Robinson, he answered right back. When a player spiked him at second, he retaliated by slapping a tag across that player's jaw the next chance he got. And if a pitcher threw *at* instead of *to* him, Robinson would push a bunt toward the first baseman and then slam the pitcher when he tried to cover the base.

But Campanella had a different approach. He just ignored the insults; after all, he had heard them as a child and had never been hurt. His father was white, he had attended integrated schools, and he had played against white athletes his whole life. He had no trouble getting along with white players on his own team and around the league.

Once or twice, however, even Campanella lost his temper. In a game in Milwaukee, Braves hurler Lew Burdette threw the ball right at Campanella— not once but twice during a single at-bat. The second brushback pitch sent the Dodger to the ground. "Now dammit, throw the ball over the plate," Campanella yelled, still sitting in the batter's box.

"Nigger, get up and hit," Burdette replied.

And with that, Campanella charged the mound. Both benches quickly emptied. Fortunately, their teammates separated the players and neither man was injured.

One thing Campanella and Robinson did share was a fierce desire to win, and the bitter losses of 1950 and 1951 inspired them to work even harder in their quest for a world championship. At the end of the 1951 season, Campanella was actually happier than he had ever been in his life—and with good reason. He had just won the MVP award, Branch Rickey had given him a raise to $23,000 for the next season, and he had purchased a liquor store in New York City. He had also bought a home and started a family with his second wife, Ruthe. If only the Dodgers could capture a World Series crown, Campanella would be one of the happiest men on earth.

But more disappointment was ahead for him and the Boys of Summer. In 1952, Campanella turned in another good year, and the Dodgers won the pennant by $4\frac{1}{2}$ games. Again, they faced Stengel's Yanks in the World Series. The Dodgers led the Series 3 games to 2, but in Game 6 the Yankees tied the contest up with a clutch, 3–2 victory. In the final game at Ebbets Field, the Yanks were leading 4–2 in the 7th inning, when the Dodgers loaded the bases with two outs. Jackie Robinson came to bat and hit a high pop near the pitcher's mound. The wind blew it away from the Yankees' infielders. But at the last possible instant, Billy Martin, the Yankee second baseman, stabbed at the ball and gloved it inches from the ground. Brooklyn never again threatened in the game, and the Yankees were champs once more.

6

THE WORLD CHAMPION DODGERS

"**W**ait until next year," Dodgers fans were known to cry. But the 1953 season brought more of the same. Once again in the World Series it was the Dodgers against the Yankees. This time, however, the Dodgers had breezed to the National League pennant, winning 105 games and finishing 13 games ahead of the second-place Milwaukee Braves. Carl Erskine had won 20 games, Carl Furillo had batted .344, and Campanella had hit 41 home runs and 142 RBIs, two National League single-season records for a catcher that would result in his second MVP award at season's end.

Of course, the Yanks had plenty of their own superstars: sluggers Mickey Mantle and Yogi Berra, and pitchers Whitey Ford, Johnny Sain, Vic Raschi, Ed Lopat, and Allie Reynolds would be hard to beat. But when the Series got under way, a more unlikely hero emerged—Billy Martin, the scrappy Yankees second baseman. In Game 1, Martin's bases-loaded triple gave New York an early lead

Campanella chases a popped bunt by Hank Bauer in Game 3 of the 1956 World Series.

and the Yanks won, 9–5. In Game 2, Martin and Mantle each homered off Preacher Roe to give the Yanks a 4–2 victory. The Dodgers tied the Series with two wins at Ebbets Field. In Game 3, Erskine struck out a record 14 Yankees and Campanella homered. In Game 4, Duke Snider wielded the big bat. The Yanks then regrouped, however, and won the next two games—and another World Series.

"Wait 'til next year," the fans continued to chant. But 1954 was clearly not to be their year. Both the Dodgers and the Yankees watched the 1954 Series on television as the New York Giants and Cleveland Indians battled it out for the championship. The Dodgers had finished a disappointing 5 games behind the Giants.

It had been a bad year for Campanella as well. Hand injuries had limited his playing time, and his batting average slipped to .207. His one high point of the season came when he made his sixth All-Star appearance and set an all-time record for catching 55 consecutive innings in that competition.

In 1955, the Dodgers and Yankees renewed their World Series rivalry. Brooklyn ran away with the National League pennant—they finished $13\frac{1}{2}$ games in front of the Braves, while the Yankees edged out a strong Cleveland team for the American League flag. Once again, Mantle, Berra, and Ford prepared to take on the Boys of Summer in the World Series.

After just two games—both won by the Yankees—the Brooklyn fans were again saying, "Wait 'til next year." But the tone of the Series changed dramatically when the Yanks visited Ebbets Field for Game 3. Thanks to Campanella's 3 hits (one of them a homer) and 3 RBIs, plus a fine pitching performance by a young southpaw named Johnny Podres, the Dodgers stopped the Yankees and gave

their fans some cause for hope. Then the Dodgers won twice more to take a 3-games-to-2 lead. Just one more win and the championship would be theirs.

The Yanks, of course, had other plans. They won Game 6 handily, a 5–1 victory for Ford, and needed only to beat the inexperienced Podres at Yankee Stadium the next day to hand the Dodgers another bitter World Series defeat.

But Podres pitched carefully, and the Dodgers came through with timely hits. In the 4th inning, Campanella hit a double to left field and then Hodges singled him home. In the 6th, with two Dodgers on base, Campanella executed a perfect sacrifice bunt to advance the runners, and Hodges brought another run in with a sacrifice fly. The Yankees threatened in the bottom of the inning, but Dodgers left fielder Sandy Amoros made a spectacular catch on Yogi Berra's fly ball to end the uprising.

Campanella scores on his first-inning home run in the opening game of the 1955 World Series.

The score remained still 2–0, Dodgers, in the bottom of the 9th, and Podres was still pitching. He got Bill Skowron to pop out and then fanned Bob Cerv. Now it was two down and one to go. Only one man stood between the Dodgers and their long-awaited Series triumph: Elston Howard. The Yankee slugger worked the count to 2-2, and then sent a grounder toward shortstop. Reese handled the ball and threw accurately to Hodges. "Next year" had finally come, and the Dodgers were champs. Brooklynites celebrated in the streets all night long.

After the season, Campanella received his third MVP award in five years—along with a $50,000 contract, which made him the highest-paid Dodger.

Two future Hall of Famers, catchers Roy Campanella and Yogi Berra, faced each other in five World Series.

He also had a standing offer from the club to become a coach after his retirement.

In 1956, however, Campanella was again bothered by hand injuries and batted just .219. The Dodgers won another pennant, but this time it was the Yanks who came through to win the Series. Mantle, Martin, and Berra—the Dodgers' old nemesis— combined for 8 homers, and in the fifth game the Yanks' Don Larsen pitched the only perfect game in World Series history.

After the 1956 campaign, the Boys of Summer finally began to show the signs of age. In 1957, Campanella, Reese, Furillo, and Erskine all suffered injuries. Campanella caught only 100 games, and the team dropped to third place.

At the end of the season, owner Walter O'Malley surprised the baseball world by announcing that the Dodgers would desert Brooklyn for Los Angeles, a decision that broke the hearts of the Ebbets Field patrons. Their beloved team would leave town, and their grand ballpark would be demolished.

But the easygoing Campanella accepted the move west. The Los Angeles Coliseum, where the Dodgers would play, had a short left-field fence, and Campanella looked forward to aiming his bat in that direction. Having endured two injury-filled seasons, he was looking forward to a great comeback in 1958.

7

THE ACCIDENT

At 3:30 on the morning of January 28, 1958, Roy Campanella was on his way home to Glen Cove, Long Island. Two hours earlier, he had closed his store, Roy Campanella's Choice Wines and Liquors, on the corner of Seventh Avenue and 134th Street in New York City. It was a cold night, and the roads were still covered with snow and ice from a recent storm, so Campanella drove carefully. He sat behind the wheel of a rented 1957 Chevy sedan; both his family cars, a station wagon and a Cadillac, were in the repair shop.

Campanella turned off the main road and onto a winding street that led to his home. Shortly after passing his children's school, he approached an S-curve that was covered with ice. The car skidded, and Campanella hit the brakes, but the vehicle spun out of control. The Chevy's right fender caved in as it hit a telephone pole, and the car turned completely over. Because automobiles in the 1950s were not equipped with seat belts, Campanella was thrown to the floor on the passenger's side of the car. His head and neck hit the dashboard before

Following his accident, Campanella talks baseball with three of his children: (left to right) Tony, Princess, and Roy, Jr.

his body was wedged between the dash and the front seat.

Campanella did not panic or lose consciousness. Realizing that the engine was still running and there was the possibility of the car exploding, he reached toward the ignition to turn the motor off. But for some reason, he could not move his arm. He tried again and failed. "I'm paralyzed," he thought.

A few moments later, a man who lived nearby approached the scene with a flashlight. When he shone it in the car, he immediately recognized the man whose picture was so often in the newspapers. "Would you please turn the key in the ignition," Campanella said, as related in his own book *It's Good to Be Alive.* "Turn off the engine. Please. I don't want to burn to death."

Several minutes later, a policeman and an ambulance arrived. The medics worked for twenty minutes with crowbars to pry Campanella free from the wreckage. Then they placed him face-down on a stretcher and rushed him off to Glen Cove Community Hospital.

At the hospital, the doctors moved quickly. X-rays showed that Campanella's back had been broken between the fifth and sixth vertebrae. In addition, his spinal cord had been nearly severed. The doctors received permission from Roy's wife, Ruthe, to operate. A brace was attached to Campanella's head and neck to keep them rigid. Then Dr. Robert Sengstaken repaired the damaged backbone. The operation lasted four hours and saved Campanella's life.

If Campanella's car had not been found imme-diately after the accident, if the rescue team had not arrived so quickly, and if the doctors had not worked so efficiently, the pressure of the broken

Roy had his own baseball talk show, called "Campy's Corner," on WINS.

backbone on the spinal cord would have proved fatal. As it was, Campanella's recovery would be slow. Moreover, the doctors feared that his paralysis—he could move neither his arms nor lower body after surgery—would be permanent.

Dr. Sengstaken was honest with his patient and with the newspaper reporters who soon flocked to the hospital. Campanella was out of immediate danger, but there was no way of knowing how long the paralysis would last. The doctor told Campanella that he might never walk again and that he would be foolish even to think about playing baseball in the future.

Three days after his accident, Campanella contracted pneumonia, and the doctors had to work hard just to keep him breathing. A tracheotomy was performed—a hole was cut in his throat and a tube was inserted into his windpipe so he would breathe. His lungs cleared, but he spent the next 100 days flat on his back, strapped to a bed with a metal brace attached to his head and neck. He began to think that it might have been better to have died in that 1957 Chevrolet.

But Dr. Sengstaken knew his patient was not a quitter. "Roy," he said, "you've got to fight. We can only help you ten percent. The other ninety has to be your effort."

Soon afterward, Campanella began to improve. Some feeling returned to his hands, and he was able to sit up in a wheelchair. On May 5th, he was transferred to New York University's Institute of Physical Medicine and Rehabilitation, generally known as the Rusk Institute (after Dr. Howard A. Rusk, the clinic's head physician). There, Campanella worked to get some movement from his crippled body. He learned to move around in a wheelchair and to feed himself with the help of a gadget attached to his wrist. With some embarrassment, he began attending physical therapy classes. During one session, he practiced catching

Hector Torres, the star pitcher for the Monterrey, Mexico team, winners of the 1958 Little League World Series, hands Campanella a baseball to sign. Fourteen years later, Torres appeared in a game in the major leagues.

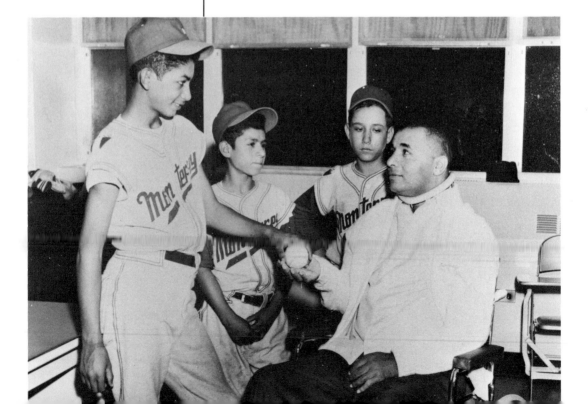

a soft white volleyball. The man who had caught some of the National League's best pitchers had to learn again how to catch a ball.

Campanella became the Rusk Institute's leading cheerleader. When a patient was depressed, Campanella wheeled himself over and delivered a pep talk. One middle-aged man who had lost a leg in an automobile accident would not cooperate in his rehabilitation. He had been fitted with a wooden leg, but he refused to stand on it; instead, he sat all day in a wheelchair crying and feeling sorry for himself.

"You think you're the unluckiest man in the world because a little thing like that has happened to you," Campanella told him. "But you're wrong. You're a lucky man. Just think how much worse off you could be. My goodness, I'd give a million to be in the condition you're in. You can walk. Man, how can you sit there in a wheelchair when you can just get up and walk is beyond me. Why, you can walk right out of here if you've a mind to. All by yourself without having to depend upon anybody else."

Campanella kept after him for two weeks. Soon, the man began to walk on his wooden leg. A short time later he left the Rusk Institute—walking on his own with the help of a cane.

Campanella remained at the Rusk Institute for six months, receiving a never-ending stream of visitors and well-wishers. Carl Erskine, Pee Wee Reese, and other Dodger teammates came by. Branch Rickey stopped in, and so did many other baseball people—including Lew Burdette, the pitcher who had insulted Campanella a few years earlier.

Campanella wasted no time feeling sorry for himself. Even before he left the Rusk Institute, he had already begun his next career. He contracted to conduct a radio interview show featuring himself and various sports celebrities. Pee Wee Reese, boxer Sugar Ray Robinson, Yankees shortstop Phil Rizzuto and Yogi Berra, and Branch Rickey were among the guests on what became known as "Campy's Corner." During the 1958 World Series, Campanella was allowed to leave the institute to attend three World Series games at Yankee Stadium and write about them for a newspaper chain.

A short time before Campanella went home for good, a press conference was held to inform the public of his progress. "He has worked so hard to accomplish the things he has that he has been an inspiration to us all," Dr. Rusk told the reporters. "This is hard to say, but I honestly believe that Roy's contribution to this life has been far greater than anything he could possibly contribute to it through baseball. The way he has been able to combat this misfortune has given hope to so many, many thousands of disabled persons, not only in this country, but all over the world. I believe he actually has become a symbol to them. We know that from all the letters we have received."

Campanella returned home on November 7, 1958, still paralyzed. He continued to operate his liquor store and to host "Campy's Corner." In March 1959, at the Dodgers' invitation, he flew to Vero Beach to coach the team's young catcher, Johnny Roseboro. And early in the season, on May 7th, they held "Roy Campanella Night" at the Los Angeles Coliseum. Some 93,103 fans—the largest crowd ever to attend a baseball game—paid tribute to the man who had helped the team win five National League pennants.

But life never got easy for Campanella. He remained in a wheelchair, unable to move anything but his arms and hands. In 1960, his wife, Ruthe,

who had helped him recover from the accident, left him and he filed for divorce. Struggling for money, he was forced to sell their house at auction.

Fortunately, Campanella was able to cope with these tragedies; in fact, they seemed to make him stronger. He moved into an apartment in Harlem to be close to his business. In 1964, he married a neighbor named Roxie Doles, and they bought a comfortable home in the nearby suburb of White Plains. He watched his six children, two from his first marriage and four from his marriage to Ruthe, grow into productive adults, and he worked for the Dodgers during spring training. In 1969, he was elected to the Baseball Hall of Fame.

When writer Roger Kahn interviewed Campanella in 1970, Roy said that he was satisfied with his life. "I've accepted the chair," he said. "My family has accepted it. My wife has made me a wonderful home. I'm not wanting many things. Sure, I'd love to walk. Sure, I would. But I'm not gonna worry myself to death because I can't. I've

Even after his accident, Roy worked with the Dodger players at Vero Beach, the team's training complex in Vero Beach, Florida. From left: Norm Miller, Steve Yeager, Joe Ferguson, Bill Russell, Manny Mota, and Campanella.

Roy is assisted by Walter Alston and the Yankees' Casey Stengel at a game honoring Campanella. The May 7, 1959, crowd at the Los Angeles Coliseum was 93,103, the largest in baseball history.

accepted the chair, and I've accepted life."

In 1978, the Campanellas moved to California. The former catcher joined his longtime teammate Don Newcombe on the Dodgers' Community Service Team. In the years that followed, Campanella made speaking appearances for the Dodgers throughout southern California and served as a catching instructor when the club went to Florida for spring training. During the regular season, he attended every home game and rooted passionately for the "new" Dodgers.

"He had never hit bottom," former teammate Carl Erskine said in a recent interview. "Where's he get that strength? Well, I've asked myself that so many times." It's a question that has no easy answer. Those who know Roy Campanella think he may get some of his strength from looking back at his accomplishments: winning three MVP awards, playing for five pennant-winning teams, catching in seven major-league All-Star games. But Campanella probably gets even greater satisfaction when he looks at the baseball diamonds of today and sees black ballplayers on every team— and even black managers in a few dugouts.

Perhaps it was another great black ballplayer, Hank Aaron, who best summarized Campanella's achievements. When Aaron and Frank Robinson were inducted into the Hall of Fame in 1982, Aaron said, "I'm proud to be standing where Jackie Robinson, Roy Campanella, and others made it possible for players like Frank Robinson and myself to prove that a man's ability is limited only by his lack of opportunity."

Roy Campanella helped open up opportunities— first for black baseball players, and then for handicapped citizens—and that is his greatest achievement.

CHRONOLOGY

Nov. 19, 1921	Roy Campanella is born in Homestead, Pennsylvania.
Spring, 1937	Signs with the Baltimore Elite Giants of the Negro National League.
1942-43	Leaves the Elite Giants to play in Mexico.
1944	Re-signs with the Elites for $3,000 per year.
1946	Signs with the Brooklyn Dodgers and plays for the club's farm team in Nashua, New Hampshire.
Apr. 15, 1947	Jackie Robinson plays his first game for Brooklyn, breaking major-league baseball's color line.
1947	Playing for Montreal, Campanella wins the league's MVP award.
May, 1948	Is sent to St. Paul in the American Association and becomes the first black to play in the league.
June 30, 1948	Promoted to Brooklyn and finishes the season with the Dodgers.
1949	The Dodgers win the National League pennant but lose the Series to the Yankees.
1951	The Dodgers blow a 13 $^{1}/_{2}$ game lead and lose to the Giants in a 3-game playoff. Campanella is named N.L. MVP.
1952	The Dodgers win another pennant and lose another Series to the Yankees.
1953	The Dodgers win the pennant and the Yankees win the Series. Campanella earns his second MVP award.
1955	The Dodgers win the pennant and the World Series. Campanella wins his third N.L. MVP trophy.
1956	The Dodgers lose their World Series crown to the Yankees.
1957	Walter O'Malley announces that the Dodgers will be moving to Los Angeles.
Jan. 28, 1958	Campanella's neck is broken and his spinal cord nearly severed in an automobile accident.
1969	Elected to the Baseball Hall of Fame.
1978	Moves to California where he continues his long association with the Dodgers.

ROY CAMPANELLA
"CAMPY"

BROOKLYN N. L. 1948 - 1957
MOST VALUABLE PLAYER N. L. 1951-1953-1955
ESTABLISHED RECORDS FOR CATCHERS: MOST
HOME-RUNS IN A SEASON 41, MOST RUNS
BATTED IN 142. SET N.L. RECORD FOR CHANCES
ACCEPTED BY CATCHERS FOR MOST CONSECUTIVE
YEARS 6, TIED RECORD FOR MOST YEARS IN
PUTOUTS 6, CAUGHT 100 OR MORE GAMES FOR
MOST CONSECUTIVE YEARS 9. LED IN FIELDING
AVERAGE FOR CATCHERS 1949-1952-1953-1957.

MAJOR LEAGUE STATISTICS

Brooklyn Dodgers

YEAR	TEAM	G	AB	R	H	2B	3B	HR	RBI	BA	SB
1948	BKN N	83	279	32	72	11	3	9	45	.258	3
1949		130	436	65	125	22	2	22	82	.287	3
1950		126	437	70	123	19	3	31	89	.281	1
1951		143	505	90	164	33	1	33	108	.325	1
1952		128	468	73	126	18	1	22	97	.269	8
1953		144	519	103	162	26	3	41	142	.312	4
1954		111	397	43	82	14	3	19	51	.207	1
1955		123	446	81	142	20	1	32	107	.318	2
1956		124	388	39	85	6	1	20	73	.219	1
1957		103	330	31	80	9	0	13	62	.242	1
Totals		1215	4205	627	1161	178	18	242	856	.276	25
World Series											
1949	BKN N	5	15	2	4	1	0	1	2	.267	0
1952		7	28	0	6	0	0	0	1	.214	0
1953		6	22	6	6	0	0	1	2	.273	0
1955		7	27	4	7	3	0	2	4	.259	0
1956		7	22	2	4	1	0	0	3	.182	0
Totals		32	114	14	27	5	0	4	12	.237	0
All Star Games (6 years)		6	18	1	2	0	0	0	0	.111	0

FURTHER READING

Ashe, Arthur T. *A Hard Road to Glory: A History of the African American Athlete.* Vols. 2 & 3. New York: Warner Books, 1988.

Barber, Red. *When All Hell Broke Loose.* New York: Doubleday, 1982.

Campanella, Roy. *It's Good to Be Alive.* Boston: Little, Brown, 1959.

Holway, John. *Blackball Stars.* Westport, CT: Meckler, 1988.

Kahn, Roger. *The Boys of Summer.* New York: Harper & Row, 1971.

Peterson, Robert. *Only the Ball Was White.* Englewood Cliffs, NJ: Prentice-Hall, 1970.

Robinson, Jackie. *I Never Had It Made.* New York: G. P. Putnam, 1972.

Tygiel, Jules. *Baseball's Great Experiment: Jackie Robinson and His Legacy.* New York: Oxford University, 1983.

Voigt, David Q. *American Baseball.* Vol. 3. University Park: Pennsylvania State University, 1983.

INDEX

PICTURE CREDITS

AP/Wide World Photos: pp. 2, 8, 11, 14, 30, 36, 42, 45, 46, 48, 51, 55, 56, 58; Courtesy of James Charlton: p. 40; Nashua Library, Nashua, NH: p. 34; National Baseball Library, Cooperstown, NY: pp. 21, 24, 33, 38, 52, 60; Temple University: pp.17, 27; UPI/Bettmann: p. 18

JAMES TACKACH teaches in the Humanities Division at Roger Williams College in Bristol, Rhode Island. He is co-author of *Great Athletes of the 20th Century*, and his articles have appeared in the *New York Times*, *The Providence Journal*, *Sports History*, and a variety of academic journals. He lives in Narragansett, Rhode Island.

JIM MURRAY, veteran sports columnist of the *Los Angeles Times*, is one of America's most acclaimed writers. He has been named "America's Best Sportswriter" by the National Association of Sportscasters and Sportswriters 14 times, was awarded the Red Smith Award, and was twice winner of the National Headliner Award. In addition, he was awarded the J. G. Taylor Spink Award in 1987 for "meritorious contributions to baseball writing." With this award came his 1988 induction into the National Baseball Hall of Fame in Cooperstown, New York. In 1990, Jim Murray was awarded the Pulitzer Prize for Commentary.

EARL WEAVER is the winningest manager in Baltimore Orioles history by a wide margin. He compiled 1,480 victories in his 17 years at the helm. After managing eight different minor league teams, he was given the chance to lead the Orioles in 1968. Under his leadership the Orioles finished lower than second place in the American League East only four times in 17 years. One of only 12 managers in big league history to have managed in four or more World Series, Earl was named Manager of the Year in 1979. The popular Weaver had his number 5 retired in 1982, joining Brooks Robinson, Frank Robinson, and Jim Palmer, whose numbers were retired previously. Earl Weaver continues his association with the professional baseball scene by writing, broadcasting, and coaching.

FREE PUBLIC LIBRARY UNION, NEW JERSEY

3 9549 00 44 3802

TOWNSHIP OF UNION
FREE PUBLIC LIBRARY